Praying the Rosary
with
MARY

BY ANGELA M. BURRIN - ILLUSTRATED BY MARIA CRISTINA LO CASCIO

Introduction

I am Mary, the mother of Jesus, and I love hearing children pray the rosary! I'm so happy that you are going to pray it with me now. Together we will be thinking about my Son, Jesus. But first, let me ask you a few questions.

Do you have a rosary of your own? Maybe you have been given a rosary for your First Holy Communion. If not, perhaps you could ask your mom or dad to take you to a religious store to buy one. That would be a fun outing!

Do you know how to pray the rosary? Begin by making the Sign of the Cross and then say the Apostles' Creed while holding the crucifix. On the short strand, start with an Our Father and three Hail Marys and end with a Glory Be. Then choose to pray one of the four sets of "mysteries"—the Joyful, Luminous, Sorrowful, or Glorious. Say the mystery, then pray an Our Father, ten Hail Marys, and a Glory Be. Then go to the next mystery. When you get to the medal on your rosary after the five decades are completed, you can pray Hail, Holy Queen. All these prayers are on the opposite page.

Did you know that little children can pray the rosary too? But they don't have to always pray all ten Hail Marys. The most important thing for anyone who is praying the rosary is to think about Jesus and pray a Hail Mary (or two or three) from their heart. And everyone who prays the rosary will receive many blessings! So let's begin!

Prayers of the Rosary

THE SIGN OF THE CROSS

In the name of the Father, and of the Son, and of the Holy Spirit. Amen.

APOSTLES' CREED

I believe in God, the Father almighty, Creator of heaven and earth,
and in Jesus Christ, his only Son, our Lord, who was conceived by the Holy Spirit,
born of the Virgin Mary, suffered under Pontius Pilate, was crucified, died and was
buried; he descended into hell; on the third day he rose again from the dead;
he ascended into heaven, and is seated at the right hand of God the Father almighty;
from there he will come to judge the living and the dead.
I believe in the Holy Spirit, the holy catholic Church, the communion of saints,
the forgiveness of sins, the resurrection of the body, and life everlasting. Amen.

OUR FATHER

Our Father, who art in heaven, hallowed be thy name; thy kingdom come,
thy will be done on earth as it is in heaven. Give us this day our daily bread,
and forgive us our trespasses, as we forgive those who trespass against us;
and lead us not into temptation, but deliver us from evil. Amen

HAIL MARY

Hail Mary, full of grace, the Lord is with you! Blessed are you among women,
and blessed is the fruit of your womb, Jesus. Holy Mary, Mother of God,
pray for us sinners, now and at the hour of our death. Amen.

GLORY BE

Glory be to the Father and to the Son and to the Holy Spirit.
As it was in the beginning, is now and ever shall be—world without end. Amen.

HAIL, HOLY QUEEN

Hail, holy Queen, Mother of Mercy, our life, our sweetness, and our hope.
To you do we cry, poor banished children of Eve. To you do we send up our sighs,
mourning and weeping in this valley of tears. Turn, then, most gracious advocate,
your eyes of mercy toward us and after this our exile, show unto us the blessed fruit
of your womb, Jesus, O clement, O loving, O sweet Virgin Mary. Pray for us,
O Holy Mother of God, that we may be made worthy of the promises of Christ.

The Annunciation

As we begin these Joyful Mysteries of the rosary, let me tell you about a very special day in my life. I was in my home in Nazareth when an angel suddenly appeared. The angel, who was named Gabriel, said, "Greetings, Mary! Don't be afraid. Your heavenly Father is pleased with you. You are to give birth to a son, and you are to name him Jesus."

I asked the angel, "How will this happen?" He said, "The Holy Spirit will come upon you. The baby will be called holy, Son of the Most High." I knew from the Scriptures that God had promised to send a Messiah to be the savior of the world.

My heart was full of joy. I wanted whatever my heavenly Father wanted. I said, "Yes, I am the Lord's servant! Let it happen as you say."

Our Father wanted to save the world through Jesus, and he asked me to say yes to that plan. How happy I am that he chose me!

Mary, every day, my heavenly Father also gives me chances to say yes to him. Pray that I will always say yes as you did!

Hail Mary …

The Visitation

Here's another thing the angel Gabriel told me: My cousin Elizabeth was also going to have a baby! So I packed my bags, gathered some food, and hurried from Nazareth down to the hill country where Elizabeth lived with her husband, Zechariah.

When Elizabeth heard my voice, her baby leapt for joy in her womb. She was filled with the Holy Spirit, and in a loud voice she cried out, "Blessed are you among women and blessed is the child you are carrying. But why am I so favored to have a visit from my Lord?" Both Elizabeth and her baby—John the Baptist—knew that Jesus was the Savior of the world!

I was so joyful that I prayed, "My soul glorifies the Lord, and my spirit rejoices in God my Savior. From now on, people will call me blessed, for the Mighty One has done great things for me."

I stayed with Elizabeth about three months. Then I returned home. Joseph and I were married, and we planned for the arrival of this special child.

Mary, how blessed you are to be God's mother!
Pray that I will always be thankful that Jesus came to earth to be with us!

Hail Mary …

The Birth of Jesus

It was a long hard ride for me on the donkey from Nazareth to Bethlehem. Because of a census, Joseph had to go to Bethlehem to register. But Joseph made sure that I rested often because I was about to have my baby.

There were so many people in the little town of Bethlehem that at first Joseph couldn't find a place for us to stay. But we both trusted our heavenly Father to take care of us. Then an innkeeper's wife showed us to a stable.

That night Jesus was born. I wrapped him in swaddling cloths. I laid him on straw in the animals' feeding manger. The ox and the donkey breathed on him to keep him warm.

Jesus' first visitors were shepherds from the hillside. An angel had appeared to them, saying, "Don't be afraid. I have such wonderful news for you! A Savior has been born. You'll find him wrapped in swaddling clothes and lying in a manger." When the shepherds found us, they were so excited!

Mary, just like you and Joseph, I want to trust my heavenly Father to always take care of me.

Hail Mary …

The Presentation

What a special day it was when Joseph and I took Jesus to the temple in Jerusalem to present him to our heavenly Father. So that we could be obedient to the Law of Moses, we took a pair of doves to offer as a sacrifice.

The Holy Spirit told a man named Simeon to go to the temple at the same time we were there. When Simeon saw Jesus, he knew that he was the Savior of the world. He took the baby Jesus in his arms and gave thanks. Joseph and I were amazed.

Then Simeon said something very startling to me: "A sharp sword will pierce your heart." I now know that he was prophesying about Jesus' terrible suffering and death on the cross.

Joseph and I also met another person in the temple, Anna. She was a widow and spent her all time there praising God. Anna told everyone the good news that the Messiah had been born.

Joseph and I then returned to Nazareth, where Jesus grew up.

Mary, pray that like Simeon and Anna,
I will always be led by the Holy Spirit.

Hail Mary …

The Finding of Jesus in the Temple

Every year Jesus, Joseph, and I went to Jerusalem for the Passover festival. When Jesus was twelve, we went to the festival as usual. After it was over, we started back home to Nazareth.

What we didn't know was that Jesus had stayed on in Jerusalem.

We traveled for a whole day before we realized that Jesus was not in the caravan with us. We asked our relatives and friends, but no one knew where he was. We were so worried!

After three long days of looking for him, we finally found Jesus in the temple. He was sitting with the Jewish teachers, listening to them and asking them questions. Everyone was amazed at his intelligent answers.

I asked Jesus, "Son, why have you done this to us?" Jesus replied, "Don't you know that I have to be in my Father's house?" I was puzzled by what he said, but we returned to Nazareth, and Jesus was obedient to us.

And I treasured all these things in my heart. I started to understand that Jesus had a very special mission.

Mary, I know that I too have a special mission.
Pray that I will do what God asks of me.

Hail Mary …

The Baptism of Jesus

These next mysteries of the rosary are called "luminous" because Jesus is the light of the world. What a light he was to all the people who saw him during his three years of preaching and healing!

In those days, many people were making their way to the River Jordan to be baptized by John the Baptist. When John lowered people into the water, they were cleansed of their sins.

Jesus came to John one day to be baptized. But John knew that Jesus was the Son of God and had no sin. So he said, "I need to be baptized by you." But Jesus replied, "No, John, let it be this way for now."

When Jesus came up out of the water, the heavens opened and the Holy Spirit came upon him like a dove. And a voice from heaven said, "This is my Son whom I love; with him I am very pleased."

What a wonderful day for my son! Now he was ready to begin telling everyone about his Father's great love for them.

Mary, I know that I am a beloved child of my Father.
Pray that I may love others the way Jesus loves me.

Hail Mary …

The Wedding at Cana

I was at a wedding in the town of Cana in Galilee. Jesus and his disciples were there too. After the wedding ceremony, we celebrated for many days. We ate, sang, and danced.

Suddenly I noticed that the wine had run out. I said to Jesus, "They have no more wine." Jesus replied, "My hour has not yet come." But I said to the servants, "Do whatever he tells you."

Jesus told the servants to fill six stone jars with water. Then he said, "Pour some out and give it to the head server." The server tasted it and said to the bridegroom, "The best wine is usually served first, and then the cheaper wine. But you have saved the best wine until now." This was Jesus' first miracle!

Just as I told Jesus about the problem with the wine, I will tell him about any of the problems you may have. So as you pray this rosary, don't hesitate to let me know what you need!

Mary, you are Jesus' mother and my mother too.
I know you care about all of my problems and needs!

Hail Mary …

Jesus Proclaims the Kingdom of God

Jesus left our home in Nazareth. He chose twelve disciples, and then spent three years telling everyone about the kingdom of God. He taught in synagogues, on hillsides, and even from boats!

And what did Jesus say? He told people that their heavenly Father loved them and wanted to have a special friendship with them. He said it pleases our Father when we are loving, kind, patient, and obedient. And he taught us to forgive anyone who hurts us.

And what did Jesus do? When Jesus saw people with terrible diseases or those who couldn't see, hear, or walk, he healed them. So many people wanted to see Jesus that he didn't have much time to eat or sleep. He even had to slip away in the middle of the night to pray.

Jesus' teaching and miracles helped people to believe that he was truly the Messiah. The kingdom of God had come!

Mary, I'm so happy that the kingdom of God is here!
Pray for me that I will tell others that Jesus loves them and wants to heal them.

Hail Mary …

The Transfiguration

Have you ever seen anything so white and bright that it glows? That's how Jesus looked at his Transfiguration!

This is what happened. One day Jesus took Peter, James, and John with him to a mountain to pray. Suddenly his face shone so brightly that it looked like the sun, and his clothes became a dazzling white. Then Moses and Elijah appeared with Jesus and talked with him.

When Peter and the other two disciples saw Jesus' glory, they were excited. Peter said, "Jesus, how good it is that we are here. Let us make three tents—one for you, one for Moses, and one for Elijah."

While Peter was speaking, a bright cloud appeared and covered them. Then they heard a voice from the cloud, saying, "This is my beloved Son. Listen to him!" The disciples were afraid, but Jesus told them not to worry.

As they came down the mountain, Jesus told them not to tell anyone about what had happened until he had risen from the dead.

Mary, in heaven everyone sees your Son's glory. I want to see it too!
Pray that my heart always longs for heaven.

Hail Mary …

The Institution of the Eucharist

Do you know how much Jesus loves you? He loves you so much that he comes to you in the Eucharist!

On the night before Jesus died on the cross, he celebrated the feast of the Passover with his disciples. During the meal, Jesus took a piece of unleavened bread, and after thanking his Father, he broke it, gave it to his disciples, and said, "Take this, all of you, and eat it. This is my body, which will be given up for you."

Then Jesus took a cup of wine and said, "Take this, all of you, and drink from it. This is the cup of my blood. It will be shed for you and for many so that sins may be forgiven. Do this in memory of me."

I am Jesus' mother. When Jesus was a baby, I held him in my arms. When he was dying, I stood at the foot of the cross. You too are close to Jesus every time you receive him in the Eucharist.

Mary, I know that it's really Jesus that I receive in the Eucharist.
Pray that I will treasure this time with him.

Hail Mary …

The Agony in the Garden

As we pray these Sorrowful Mysteries, join me in thinking about Jesus' suffering and death. After Jesus' last supper with his disciples, he took them to a garden called Gethsemane.

Jesus chose his special friends, Peter, James, and John, to be with him. "My heart is full of sadness. Stay here with me while I pray," he said.

Jesus went a little farther and knelt down to pray. He knew that the next day, he was going to die on the cross. He prayed, "Father, if it is possible, let this cup be taken away from me. But not my will, but your will be done."

Three times Jesus went back to his disciples, hoping to find them awake. But each time he found them sleeping.

Then Judas came into the garden with some soldiers. He had a plan to betray Jesus. "Arrest the man that I kiss," he had told the soldiers. So Judas kissed Jesus, and immediately the soldiers arrested him. Jesus' disciples were so afraid that they ran away. When I heard that Jesus had been arrested, I knew his suffering had begun.

Mary, pray that I will never be afraid to say that I am a friend of Jesus.

Hail Mary …

The Second Sorrowful Mystery

The Scourging at the Pillar

What happened next to my son Jesus pierced my heart!

Jesus was tied up with chains and dragged off to the Praetorium, the home of the Roman governor, Pilate. Jesus didn't struggle to get free. He was like a lamb on its way to be killed. He knew that this was all part of his Father's plan, to be the perfect lamb that was sacrificed for the sins of all.

When Pilate saw Jesus, he said, "I don't think this man has done anything wrong." He thought Jesus should be released. So Pilate asked the crowd, "Do you want me to release Barabbas, the murderer, or Jesus?" "Barabbas!" they shouted.

Several soldiers led Jesus into the courtyard. They took off his outer clothes and tied him to a pole. Then they took turns striking Jesus with leather whips. They did this many, many times.

Jesus was bleeding all over his shoulders, back, arms, and legs. He was in horrible pain, but he didn't cry out or complain.

Mary, I'm so sorry that Jesus had to suffer.
Pray that I will remember that he did this because he loves me so very much.

Hail Mary …

The Crowning with Thorns

The soldiers began making fun of Jesus. I knew he didn't deserve to be treated this way. My son had always been so kind and loving to everyone.

One soldier said, "This man says he's a king. Let's dress him up like one!" They found a purple robe and placed it over his bleeding shoulders. "A king needs a crown," another soldier said. "Let's make one out of branches." So they found branches with large thorns on them and twisted them into a crown. Then they put it on Jesus' head. They even gave him a reed to hold as if it were a king's scepter.

The soldiers started laughing at Jesus. Some got on their knees before him, saying, "Hail, King of the Jews!" Others started spitting at him. One grabbed the reed from Jesus' hand and hit him over his head with it. Blood trickled down my son's face from the crown of thorns.

After the soldiers had finished mocking Jesus, they took off the purple robe. But they left the crown of thorns on his head.

Mary, pray for me that I will never tease or make fun of people.

Hail Mary …

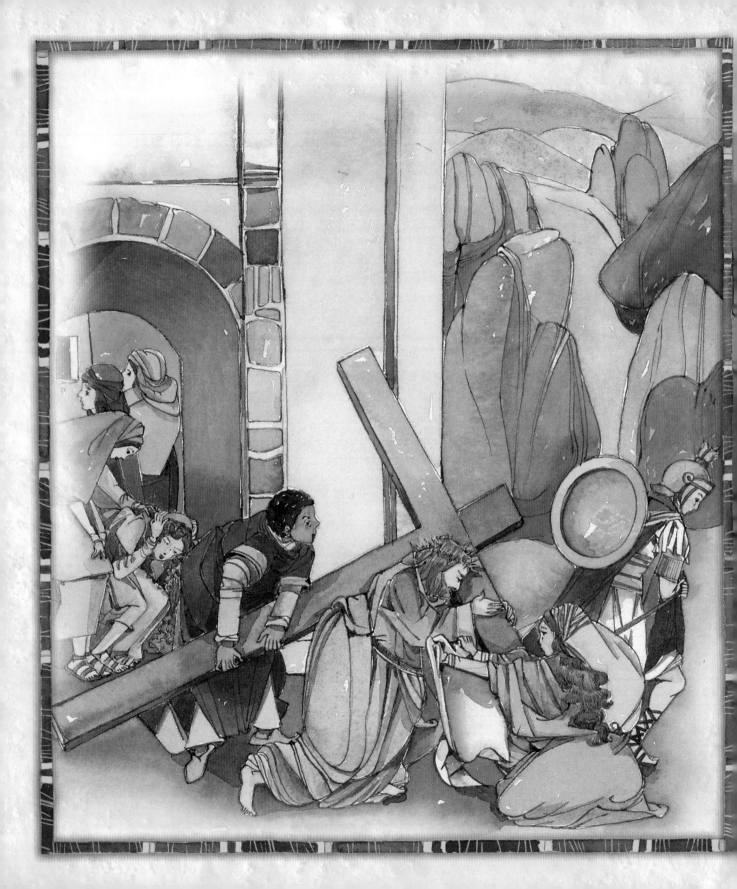

The Carrying of the Cross

What a heavy cross Jesus had to carry! Jesus dragged it for about a third of a mile along the narrow, uneven stones that paved the streets of Jerusalem. I was among the crowd of people who followed him up to Calvary, the place where criminals were crucified

Three times I saw my son fall under the weight of his cross. When the soldiers saw him fall, they said angrily, "Get up!" And then they whipped Jesus and dragged him to his feet by a cord around his waist.

Finally they realized that Jesus needed help. So they grabbed a man from the crowd. He was a foreigner, Simon of Cyrene, and he helped Jesus carry his cross.

Along the way, women were crying because they saw how much Jesus was suffering. Exhausted and hardly able to speak, Jesus stopped and said to them, "Daughters of Jerusalem, do not weep for me, but pray for yourselves and for your children."

And as Jesus carried his cross, he met me, his sorrowful mother

Mary, when my friends need help,
pray that I will go out of my way to help them.

Hail Mary …

The Crucifixion

I was with Jesus' disciple, John, as we arrived at Calvary. Now was the moment I'd been dreading. Jesus was going to be crucified.

Jesus was laid down on the cross. Soldiers hammered nails into his hands and feet. I heard his moans. Then they dropped the cross into a hole in the ground. He was between two criminals. One said to him, "Jesus, remember me when you come into your kingdom." Jesus replied, "Today you will be with me in Paradise."

It was so hard for me to see my son in such agony. But Jesus was not thinking of himself—he was thinking of me! He said to John, "Behold, your mother." Then he said to me, "Behold, your son."

From the cross Jesus said, "I thirst." A soldier gave him a sponge dipped in wine. Then his strength gave out. Jesus said, "It is finished." He bowed his head, and my beloved son died for the salvation of the world.

Mary, pray for me that I will remember every day
that Jesus died for my sins.

Hail Mary ...

The Resurrection

Jesus' death is not the end of the story. Do you know what happened? My son Jesus rose from the dead! He is alive! That's why these next mysteries are called "glorious"!

After taking Jesus down from the cross, we buried him in a tomb owned by Joseph of Arimathea. On the first day of the week, just as the sun was rising, Mary Magdalene, Salome, and Mary, the mother of James, went to the tomb to anoint Jesus' body with spices. On the way, they asked each other, "Who will roll the stone away from the entrance to the tomb?"

But just as they got there, the earth shook and the stone moved! An angel appeared and said to the women, "Have no fear! Jesus has risen! He is not here. Go and tell his disciples."

As they hurried away from the tomb, suddenly they saw Jesus! "Greetings," he said. "Do not be afraid. Go and tell my brothers to go to Galilee. There they will see me."

When the women told me this good news about Jesus, I was so happy and excited! I couldn't wait to see him again!

Mary, pray for me to tell others the good news: Jesus is alive!

Hail Mary …

The Ascension

For forty days Jesus appeared to me, his disciples, and many others. I loved being with Jesus again! Every time I saw him, my heart was filled with joy.

"Go and make disciples of everyone," Jesus said. "Baptize them in the name of the Father and of the Son and of the Holy Spirit. Teach them to obey my commandments to love God and one another."

We knew that Jesus would return to his Father in heaven. But he left us with a great promise. He said, "I am with you always, until the end of time!" So we also knew that Jesus would still be with us even when we couldn't see him any longer.

Then Jesus took his disciples to a mountain. There he ascended into heaven. His friends watched until a cloud hid him from their sight.

My son is now seated at the right hand of his Father in heaven. But Jesus is also in your heart. And you can receive him at every Mass in the Eucharist!

Mary, pray for me to know that Jesus is always with me,
even though I can't see him.

Hail Mary . . .

The Coming of the Holy Spirit

"Wait in the upper room in Jerusalem until I send you my Holy Spirit," Jesus had told his disciples before his Ascension.

Ten days later, there we were, all gathered together in the upper room. We had been praying and singing all day and all night. Suddenly a powerful wind came from heaven. The noise filled the whole room. And then something appeared like tongues of fire and rested on the heads of each one of us.

The promised Holy Spirit had come! Our hearts were filled with joy, and we began to speak in other languages. There were many foreigners listening to us, and they were surprised because they each heard what we were saying in their own language.

No longer were the disciples afraid. Peter went out into the streets and told the crowds, "Jesus is alive! He has died for your sins." The people asked, "What shall we do?" Peter said, "Repent and be baptized in the name of Jesus." And on that day, about three thousand men and women were baptized and filled with the Holy Spirit!

Mary, pray that I would remember to ask the Holy Spirit
to help me with everything I do and say.

Hail Mary …

The Assumption

I was very thankful that Jesus had asked his disciple John to take care of me. After Jesus ascended into heaven, I went to live in John's home. There I prayed for the disciples as they spread the good news all over the world.

When I died, Jesus' disciples and my friends were sad that I was no longer with them. After all, I had been their mother too. They laid my body in a tomb. But when they returned, my body was no longer there.

You see, God had a special plan for me. Because I was the mother of Jesus, I was taken, body and soul, into heaven. My assumption into heaven is a sign for you. At the end of the world, Jesus will come back and raise up your body too. How wonderful that will be!

I'm in heaven now! Remember: I'm your Blessed Mother, and I love it when you talk to me and pray my rosary

Mary, pray that I will always keep my eyes fixed on heaven
and the promise of eternal life!

Hail Mary …

The Crowning of Mary

I have been given a most wonderful gift. I have been crowned Queen of Heaven. I am queen of all the angels and saints. I am your queen too.

Imagine me dressed as brightly as the sun, with the moon under my feet and a crown of twelve stars on my head!

In heaven there is an enormous crowd. There are people from every country in the world. They are dressed in white robes and hold palm branches in their hands. Together with the angels, we all sing, praising God in a heavenly chorus. What a beautiful sound!

Every day I listen for the prayers of all the people in the world. Then I bring your requests to Jesus. He loves to listen to me. He is so pleased when you honor me.

Thank you for praying the rosary and for taking the time to think about all that Jesus has done for you. Remember, Jesus loves you, and he's always with you.

Mary, thank you for praying this rosary with me.
I look forward to joining you again in meditating on these awesome mysteries!

Hail Mary …

Published in the U.S. and Canada by
The Word Among Us Press
7115 Guilford Road
Frederick, Maryland 21704
www.wau.org

ISBN: 978-1-59325-206-9

Publishing Director: Annette Reynolds
Art Director: Gerald Rogers
Pre-production: Krystyna Kowalska Hewitt
Production: John Laister

Printed and bound in Singapore
July 2012

Nanny and Me

Copyright© 2015 by Florence Ann Romano

Requests for permission to make copies of any part of the work should be submitted online at info@mascotbooks.com or mailed to Mascot Books, 560 Herndon Parkway #120, Herndon, VA 20170.

PRT0315A

Printed in the United States
Library of Congress Control Number: 2015902742
ISBN-13: 9781620867860

www.mascotbooks.com

NANNY and ME

Florence Ann Romano

Illustrated by Sydni Kruger

To my forever babies:

Alexandra, John, Michelle, Claire, Annie, Jack, and Elin.

This book is not only *for* you, but it *is* you … all of you.

Mommies and daddies are different in every family. Some **MOMMIES** stay home and play while daddies go to work.

Other **DADDIES** stay home and play while mommies go to work. Some families have mommies and daddies who both go to work.

Both Mommy and Daddy have to work every day. It's sometimes hard saying goodbye to them and they don't like saying goodbye to me, but it also means I get to see my special friend. I call her Nanny, and she takes care of me and my brother while Mommy and Daddy are gone.

Every time I see her, she wraps me up in a big hug and asks me, "Are you ready to have a fun ADVENTURE today?"

I always say YES!

Before we can go on our adventures, we have to get dressed. NANNY helps me with my zippers and she puts a beautiful ribbon in my hair. I try to tie my own shoelaces, but sometimes it's better if NANNY helps me with that too.

One of my favorite places to visit is the zoo.
I love to see the animals and learn about
their homes and what they like to eat.
Whenever we go see the **PENGUINS**,
Nanny always makes me laugh when
she walks like the **PENGUINS** do.

Penguins

Other days, we go to the park by my house. Nanny loves to play with me on the **SWINGS**. She makes me fly high into the sky! Then we go on the see-saw and **GIGGLE** every time we touch the ground. When I go down the slide, Nanny is always there to catch me.

Sometimes I fall and scrape my knee. It hurts a lot and I sometimes cry, but Nanny has a **MAGIC KISS** to make the hurt go away. Then she reaches in her purse and covers my **BOO-BOO** with a fun Band-Aid so I can keep playing. Nanny is always ready for anything.

Sometimes, I think Nanny's purse is **MAGIC**. If I ever get hungry, she always has a granola bar or carrot sticks for me to eat.

But if my tummy really starts to rumble and tumble, Nanny knows it's time for lunch. She always makes it **SPECIAL** just for me.

If it's a hot and sunny day, we go to the pool after we eat our lunch. Nanny and I **LOVE** to swim, and she teaches me to swim like all the big kids.

She shows me how to
KICK, KICK, KICK my
legs **FAST, FAST, FAST!**
I always smile when she
makes her fishy face.

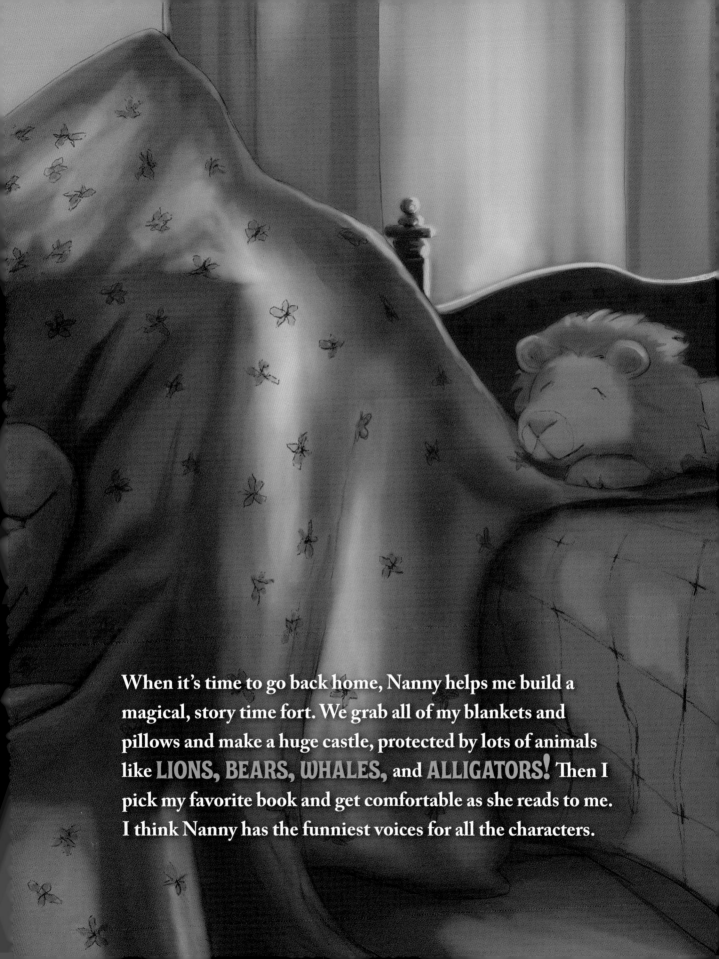

When it's time to go back home, Nanny helps me build a magical, story time fort. We grab all of my blankets and pillows and make a huge castle, protected by lots of animals like LIONS, BEARS, WHALES, and ALLIGATORS! Then I pick my favorite book and get comfortable as she reads to me. I think Nanny has the funniest voices for all the characters.

I'm pretty sleepy
after Nanny finishes
the story, so I know it's time
for a nap. I SNUGGLE up with
Nanny, and we talk about where I
want to go in my dreams. Sometimes I
jump on MARSHMALLOW CLOUDS
or take a sailboat to the moon and count all the
sparkling stars as we float by. We close our eyes really
tight and off we go!

I don't like napping for too long because I want to spend as much time with Nanny as I can! Once I wake up, we love to play GAMES. Nanny teaches me my ABCs, 1-2-3s, and all the colors of the rainbow. Nanny is so proud of me when I learn something new.

When Mommy and Daddy come home, they give me a big kiss and ask me about my day. I tell them all about my adventures and how much fun Nanny and I had. I love Mommy and Daddy, but when they come home, that means it's time for Nanny to go. She gives me a big hug goodbye and says to me, "OUR TIME HAS COME TO PART, BUT UNTIL TOMORROW, YOU ARE IN MY HEART!"

At night, I dream about flying through the sky on marshmallow clouds, waiting for tomorrow when **NANNY** will arrive once again.

About the Author

As a dedicated philanthropist, business owner, and former nanny, Florence Ann Romano has always kept a special place in her heart for children. She began caring for kids before she was a teenager and continued through a portion of adulthood. Each child that came into her life shaped her heart. Those experiences inspired her to write this book – illustrating her favorite memories, while also preparing children (and their parents) for a nanny to come into their lives. The children in this book are a combination of all her "kids," and the little boy was specially created in the image of her younger brother, who has Autism. Romano currently lives in Chicago where she remains in close contact with each child she cared for.

www.florenceannromano.com